To Dr. Howard Jones

My thanks for all the care and support given me during the last eight years —

Harriet Foley
November 26, 2013

The Butterfly Tree

Harriet Foley

Copyright 2013 Harriet Foley

All rights reserved by the author. No part of this publication may be reproduced, stored in a retrieval system, or transmitted in any form or by any means - electronic, mechanical, photocopy, recording or any other - except brief quotations in printed review, without the prior permission of the author.

Book design by Eveready Press

ISBN: 978-0-9858365-5-9

Printed in the USA

EVEREADY PRESS
Nashville, Tennessee

~ Dedication ~

*For Jonathan Joseph Foley, Jr.
who encouraged me
in whatever I attempted.*

~ Preface ~

This book of "poetry" is being published for my daughter and son-in-law, Betty and Frank Wentworth, grandchildren Ashley and Ward Waltemath, Beth Waltemath and David Lewicki, Mary Margaret Waltemath, Jonathan "Jay" Foley IV and Mitchell Foley and a few close friends.

It was written during a twelve year period as a member of the Creative Writing Class at Centennial Club. I wish to acknowledge that class and thank Dean Victor Judge of the Vanderbilt Divinity School for his guidance and encouragement during that time.

The "Chemo Chatter" poems were written during seventeen months of chemotherapy and are expressions of my gratitude as well as a tribute to Dr. Howard Jones III and nurses Bonnie Kish and Susan White of Vanderbilt Medical Center. Their support and these rhymes made a difficult time easier.

The Butterfly Tree

Purple blossoms welcoming
Yellows darting, pausing,
Tasting, taking flight
With the beat of wings.
Returning for a sip,
Extending greetings to the King,
Robed in black and royal blue.
Small greys moving in obedience
Caressing each purple hue
With a fleeting touch.
There's not much time.
Before blooms turning brown
Foretelling chill replacing heat.
All moving onward
Their cycle to complete.

~ Contents ~

The A, B, C, D, E, Fs of Harriet Foley

Aging 1

Bemusings 15

Chemo Chatter 41

Doggerel 61

Experiences 69

Family and Friends 87

Aging

Imprisoned

Won't you let my insides out?
Are you blind?
Can't you see
The dancing and romancing
Inside of me?

Shuttered by years and doubt,
Soaked in brine and put on the shelf
Outside, I wrinkle
Inside, I twinkle.
Listen, are you deaf,
Can't you hear my shout -
Let my insides out?

Evolving

Old age is not a reward
For playing by the rules,
Nor is it a penance
Deserving ridicule.

Old age is just a phase
Where cells diminish,
A stage – as to begin –
    was then -
        is now –
            the end -
But not the finish.

Tea with Betty

Now that I am old
- and purple looks bad on me –
I try to wear what I am told
When you invite me out for tea.

Should I wear a pants-suit
To hide the varicosities of blue,
Or a button-down-the front dress
As you would have me do?

Should I paint my toenails,
Wear sandals - you say's the style
Or put on my lace-up oxfords
So I can stand or walk a mile?

I have to draw my eyebrows,
Hide the brown spots on my face,
 Wear my support hose,
Remember to keep my place.

It used to be so easy-
I would put on a dress,
 Then be ready to roam,
I think I'll put my robe back on,
    and stay at home.

Age Adage

Can't find my glasses,

Or my hearing aids,

My fingers cry when I try

To pen a page.

Can't write, can't see, can't hear.

If I'm not responsive,

It's my age.

Age Adage #2

I told my friends when I grew old

I planned to be lean, mean and rich,

My friends tell me I made one –

They won't tell me which.

Age Adage #3

I know what porous means,

It's speaking of my mind,

I can still add and subtract

It's the answer I can't find...

Tempus Fugit

Old age is growing inside me

I catch a glimpse as I

    Pass the glass.

I don't stop to watch

The growth that's steady,

 Since my brain denies

    I'm ready…

Senile Lamentia

Aunt Fannie, who was about the age
  That I now am,
Would lose her glasses,
    Her keys,
    Her purse;
But never forgot the Good Book,
    Every page,
    Every chapter,
    Every verse.
While searching she would stop
    And say, "My soul hath them
    still in remembrance, and is
    humbled in me."
    "This I recall in my mind
    therefore I have hope."

I would giggle behind my hand
    So she couldn't see, but
She would turn and say,
      "Lamentations, Chapter Three."

Nowadays, when I've lost my glasses
    My keys,
    My hearing aid—
Without which no sound
 can be heard—
I plead to the muse
As I sit down to write
And search for a word.

But Paul comes to me,
    "The word is nigh thee,
    even in thy mouth
    and in thy heart."
And my own lamentation is
Why can't I find it in my mind
So my fingers can start?

The Winner

Never mind that once there was beauty,
Vibrancy, vitality and pluck,
Never mind there was veracity.
Talent and a fair share of luck,
There was wisdom – equal to a sage
But none could compete with
The irrelevance of age.

Time Was

Once there were no spots
  on my skin
Once there was no
  sagging chin,
Once my hair was
  long and brown
Once I could hear
  every sound –
  Without an aid.

No more the once
  wasp-like waist
Which hips and tummy
  have replaced.
My skin has
  a patriotic hue,
The varicosities have
  turned it red and blue.
I can't remember
  the bills I've paid.

The curl once on
  on my head
Landed on my
  fingers instead.
The eyes, once
  clear
Now drip with
  tears.
I wonder why
  they're called
  The golden years.

An Elegy to an Aging Brain

My mind has lost a million things—
Names and places,
Where my glasses are,
The dates of Presidents and Kings.

Sometimes I can't remember
The last news I heard,
But what I miss the most
Is when I can't recall a word.

So, Victor, love, at the risk
Of sounding a bit vain-glorious,
I cannot write a single line
Without a dictionary or thesaurus!!

Value Plus

My grandfather's watch fob
Is hung with an amethyst stone,
My great-grandmother's tureens
I have taken for my own,
The corner cupboard, the china closet,
   the Jackson Press,
Bring comments of their worth
   and of their age.

There is a puzzle I must confess
The answer I cannot see –
If years have brought them value
Why haven't they brought it to me?

Bemusings

Christmas Past

The house is filled with quiet
The children's chatter has gone –
No more laughs or tears,
No more Red Nose song

They came with outstretched hands,
Bearing gifts of five-by-sevens,
  Shutterflies, an eight-by-ten –
The tabletops, already filled,
Are galaxies of my kin.

"Can we have banana pudding?"
"And macaroni and cheese?"
"That's cool" replaced "thank you",
But they learned the power of "please".

They have returned
 To New York City,
  To Chicago, Decatur,
  To the Western shore.
I don't like the silence –
I need the slamming of door.

 Yes, the house reverberates with quiet –
The time went by too fast,
Again, I think this year
Was better than the last.

Creation

Wonder is a wondrous word
One with many meanings –
To think, to marvel,
To want to know,
To feel delight –
 The seven Great Wonders
  of the world
Or Aurora Borealis' light.
And then every child of every man.
With the greatest wonder of all,
The how, the when, the why
It all began.

Woman Alone

I talk daily to me,
I say, "You must send
   A check to AT&T
Piedmont Gas is overdue,
I don't want them
   To shut off the heat,
I'll get the flu.
I have to go to the grocery,
   and get some cocktail sauce,
If not, the shrimp's a total loss.

I have an internal conversation,
"I mustn't forget Charlie's visitation.
My friends are all dropping
   like flies
Pretty soon it'll be me
   Receiving the cries.
I bet Betty's ready to swap roles.
   But I can't give up control - not yet."

I lie on the sofa and look at the clouds,
"Why, there's a Rorschach blot,
It's cream that didn't clot
No - it's a shroud.
Wait, it's beginning to flee."
Daily, I talk to me,
   There's no one else to hear
At least no one I see.

Let Me Count the Days

How many winds have whipped the windows
    And slowed my pace?
How many rains have licked the panes
    And rolled down my face?
How many suns have shimmered the glass
    And brightened my space?
So many,
I cannot trace.

As the days grow late-
Whether pleasant or rough-
No matter the number
They're not nearly enough

The Fall

I am pulled
In different directions
And marvel -
Sometimes in horror -
At my selections.

I am dragged along
By strange new forces
That govern me —
Desire or rationale
Will be the sources
 From which I choose.
I see what's right
And know I approve -
But settle for pleasure
Rather than reason
And duty's call -
Then with a twinge of guilt
Complete my fall.

Germination

An embryo of a thought
Tiptoes through the fog
Hovering in my head
Looking for the essence
To fill the elliptic space
In the idea I want said.
Then, as if heaven-sent,
I feel the jolt,
The bolt of the Ah Ha
And suddenly say
Exactly what I meant

There Is No Place Called Away

There is no place called away...
I read this, wondering,
As I picked up the aerosol can
To give my hair a spray.

I'll turn on the TV
To get the news of the world,
To see what new disasters
 Providence has unfurled.

The volcanic ash from Chile
Floating over the mountains,
Landing willy-nilly,
In Argentina.

The tsunamis in Japan,
 In Indonesia -killing thousands,
Affecting the economy
In every land.

Tornados in Joplin,
That have not stopped with
Death and destruction
In Alabama.

A new volcano in Germany,
Fires in Arizona,
Arctic ice melting,
Levees failing in Missouri.

Such devastation at this great rate
Gives me a chill.
I know – I'll light the coal
I've placed in my grate.

'There is no place called away'
I wonder what the writer –
Sounds like some 'kook' -
Meant to say. .

Fame

Dunkirk, Croatia, Inchon,
Fallujah, Kuwaiti, Saigon-
Sounds that musically roll
 from the tongue
Like notes on a recorder
Until I consider the toll.

What was lost under the heap –
 the cancer cure we cannot reach.
 the unpainted picture,
 the unwritten word,
 the symphony
 that will not be heard?

Auschwitz, Hiroshima, the Afgans,
Seoul, Baghdad, Pearl, the Kurds-
Today's count, the body bags,
Replaced with folded flags
And audacious sympathy words.

I trace the carvings
On the marble monument -
I came to search a name -
I touch the cold stone
to honor the fallen.
Is this where the old
send the young
to find fame?

I no longer weep.
My tears are the tombs
And the secrets they keep.

Disclosure

I'll put on a new face
for today
I'll add some blush
to cover the gray.

I'll wear my blouse
of brightest blue
With a touch of scent
when I visit you.

I'll plump up my hair
and give it a spray
and hope that nothing
gives me away.

Descant

When I am asked how
I began writing poems
I think of my mother
And how she would gather
My sister Evelyn and me
At her knee, and proclaim,
"Today, we'll rhyme,
You both know the game".

Then she would say,
"Where are you going, Mr. Jay?"
Then I, "Far away, far away"
And Ev, Out to play, out to play".
She then,

"Where are you going Mr. Dove?"
Then I, "Up above, up above"
And Ev, "To look for love,
 To look for love."
Mr. Crow went below,
The cowbird to follow the herd.

Replacing that knee
To sit at the feet
Of Donald Davidson and
 Susan B. Riley,
Who opened the door
To Ransom, Elliot and Tate
And washed my brain
With simile and metaphor,
To give up the rhyme
And hang out my line
With my sardonic slant.
But still I can't
Forget the chant,
"Where have you gone, Mama dear?
Wish you were here,
Wish you were here."

Loss

Dark night
Does not descend.
It rises from
The ground of being up

Pulling focus from
 the eye
To no longer see
The sun or moon,
Stripping the stars
 from the sky.

Images recorded
 now unreal,
Lost in the black,
That no tears
can bring back.

Upon Reading Frost

When did the poet
Begin to ignore
Poetry's old didactic chore
To refine, explain, explore?

When did psychiatric worry
And the sound of the random word
Take their toll
On what we heard?

Lose to the ear and the air
The orderly, metered,
rhymed and spare
examination of experience—-

To leave behind
beauty versus thought,
soul versus mind.

Harm's Way

Violence encircling the globe,
Nuclear missiles made to destroy,
Terrorists' rattling, threatening stance
Demanding us to dance to their tunes.

New diseases for which we've
found no answer,
Drug wars, poverty, unemployment,
No cure for aids, madness.
    or cancer.
Racism not yet relegated to
    the rear,
Still as a nation, we persevere.

But one personal dart across
    a room
With a single venomous drop,
 Darkens the world, sets
    the heart ajar
 Leaving the self with a scar.

Grief

It does not tiptoe in on small feet
but thunders with horses hooves,
and resounds in the recesses
of the being, without bounds.

These are not the first footfalls
to stir the dust,
Leaving a silence which sears the soul
Not the only tears I have shed
to slake the thirst.
For some, silence is no solace,
Nor does weeping
fill the gapping hole.

The cliches are many—
"this too shall pass", "life goes on",
"he wouldn't want",
"it's all in your attitude".
But my friends, the one about
the perfection of practice
remains a platitude.

I Worry

I worry,
Because our culture became more materialist,
Leaving less room for those things
That enrich our days.

I worry,
Because we become
More and more critical,
Leaving less room for praise.

I worry,
That the leaders of the world
Can never forget themselves to solve
The pressing problems of poverty or peace.

I worry,
That the world does not have enough resources
To sustain the population's growth,
Is war the only answer or can resources increase?

I worry,
About the hopefuls who come
To our shores to find a better way,
 Then are sent from this home of immigrants.

I worry,
About what man is doing to the earth.
The mountains, the plains, the sea, the air.
 Can we find a useful discriminant?

I worry,
As the number of non-believers grow,
Betraying ourselves, deserting our churches,
Who will relieve us of our strife?

I worry,
If a large meteor should hit the earth,
What will happen to this planet's life?

I worry,
Because that's what I do.
…and someone needs to.

Revelation

The closer I get to dying
The church seems more surreal
Yet I keep trying
To find one with more appeal.

I believe the ultimacy of God,
Have known the Holy Spirit,
But now I'd rather feel it, see it, do it,
Than have to sit and hear it.

The fabric of my days
Goes from flour-sacks to silk,
I've had the good earth, the Good Book,
Anglicanism,
And an Existential look.

In retrospect,
The religious life I've led
Looks like a crazy quilt-
Patches faggoted by a thread,
Knotted with my mother's guilt

I have put that quilt in storage,
The new comforter dispels the chill,
I no longer forage,
I am content with His will

A Place to Come from*
for Evelyn

Next to the peony garden
Separated by the privet hedge,
You stood, giving shelter
As you had for more than
A hundred years, your girth
Now as large as your years
Of birth.

Your roots were rivulets
Of bark,
Made smooth by pushing through
The earth and bathed by seasons
Of snow and rain.

They offered two little girls
A place to play, to learn to know
To love and become what
They were to be - to deal
With joy and know of pain.

The roots were rooms for
Their paper dolls,
Kitchens for their concoctions
Storage for their treasures, and
A school to learn of nature's gifts.

Your roots anchored the quilts
The girls sneaked to lie on and
Gaze through your elliptical leaves,
That looked golden with glimpses
Of blue showing through;
And Yellow Finch, and red Cardinals, and

Blue Jays stealing your berries.
With the raucous row of the
Red-winged Blackbird, leaving the
Girls gifts, unasked and unwanted,
To let them know that life
Is sometimes absurd.

Your bough held the rope
That with a push and a pump
Took them to the sky, above
The peonies and the privet, to
Reach for the clouds – then
To let the "cat die".

Some call the hackberry a "trash tree"
With your rough bark, soft yellow wood,
And trunk knotted with numerous
Narrow limbs.
To two little girls you were
The place they practiced what
Would become their molds;
And learn to love nature's
Primary colors, that continue
To feed their souls.

*Apologies to Robert Penn Warren

A Place Revisited

Last week, on a visit,
My brother Jesse
Suggested I ride
To see if my tree
Still held its place
In the country-side.

The lane I traveled,
  now paved
  once graveled—
familiar, yet with a different face ,
  cedars gone, holly now tall,
   small houses filling the space
    where once we roamed,
   to run, to hide,
   to climb, to fall —
Ended, so I could see
If there still stood
My hackberry tree.

Oh, you still stand
But so forlorn,
With limbs that once
Shone green and yellow
Or in winter wore an ermine dress,
Now downcast, bare and shorn
For lines bringing that
Paradox called progress.

Your once strong trunk, now peeling gray,
Roots scored by the mower's blade
Where once two young girls
   came to play.
No boughs with berries
  for birds of red or blue,
   no chirp of a chickadee,
But the callous caw of the crow
As he peered down with beady eye,
  before he, too, flew.

As I glanced at my own gnarled
  digits and broken limb
   I clutched my cane.
 With memories etched
in bark, thought of what is,
not knowing what is yet to be,
I am struck by the eerie
  synchronicity
Of my tree and me.

Transcendence

I listen to your voice

And hear the words unspoken

I watch your face

See the subtle change –

A token of your past self –

As you wander

To another time and place.

Can the two of us

Transcend this new role

Put aside the pain and fears

And once again be fully whole?

A Kidnapping

As you sit at the table
        with me,
Your eyes dart
        across the space
As if looking for
        another face.
Perhaps you only view
        the crisp fall air.
Still, you have gone
        ...... somewhere.

Where are you -
Can you not see
You have also taken
A part of me?

Global Warming

Man's plan was to remake the earth
Steam and smoke
Drills and dynamite
Chemicals and concrete
Bricks and bulwarks
Ingenious tractors
Removing mountaintops
Felling forests primeval.
Nuclear reactors.
And man said, "See the progress I have brought,
Look at me."

For the God of Genesis had written it was His plan
For man to remake the earth. And man believed.

Earth's mirth at man's audacity,
With much perspicacity, caused
Quaking faults
Crushing waves
Twisting winds
Pounding rains
Flooding plains
Gobbling glaciers
Drying lands
Breaking bricks and plaster.
Natural disasters.

And the earth said, "See what I have wrought.
Leave me be."

Then the earth quoted the God of Psalms,
"Give us help from trouble, for vain is the help of man."
She begged, "Please, let him leave me be."

Critical Aclaim

The new critics made the decision
That poets must write with precision.
They also say emphatically,
If poets wish to write problematically,
They must do so precisely
Or have the critics say nicely,
That they won't wax ecstatically
Instead they'll express their derision.

Chemo Chatter

Some Doggerel for Dr. Jones

My name is Ishmael,
I'm the great white shark
Cast by Dr. Jones
Into my Hostess' lair
To catch the tenacious C-Cells
Swimming there.

She cried, "Yes", "Whoopee", "Right on",
Until she found
I was going to eat her hair!

Thanks to Dr. Jones for the imagery.
Apologies to Herman Melvin for misuse of character.
Deepest apologies to anyone who reads this.
                                    — hf

Chemotherapy Patient

Plop – pause – plop – pause – plop
The one-eyed monster drops the toxin
Into the clear tube
To flood the blood
At the port of the waiting arm.

The patient watching,
 Dry-eyed, the slow flow
  Of the infusion,
 Wondering why this intrusion
   is borne
Thinking of the forlorn days following
Conjuring how to cope
Answering the why
With the sheer possibility
Of added months and years –
  a speculative hope –
Lending credence to Cyclops' tears.

We'll See

I wonder how I will be
If the doctor says to me
You again have ovarian III.

Will I be stoic
      Not shed a tear?
Will I be heroic
      And show no fear?

Will I endeavor
      To live each day
As if I will never
Pass away?

Or will it bring out
      The very worst
As I weep and wail
      And feel I'm cursed?

Perhaps I'll give thanks
      For the care I've been shown
Then settle in peace
      With the love I've known.

Yes, I wonder how I will be.

We'll just have to wait and see.

The Shark and Harriet

I am Ishmael
I am catching cells
Both bad and good
She says, with joy,
Yes you should,
for I am without
a strand of hair
And you have left
Across my derriere
A herpes zoster trail,
But I am not bereft
  though you have won the toss
Both the head and tail!

  So yes, I say go, I know you're right
I put my fate in the good hands
Of Dr. Jones and Nurse White!

Neuropathy

Ishmael is my name
I'm the shark
Cruising the patient's frame
Searching for cancer cells –
In the daylight
And in the dark

I look
Up and down
Left and right,
Though no c-cells
Are in sight
I pause to take a bite.

The patient's left extremity
Is my favorite feeding ground
Although a remedy
Is what she hopes is found.

But think of the Ahabs,
A captain and a king,
Neither one could win.
Whales and sharks are brothers-
Evolutionary leg men!

Seventeen Months of Chemotherapy

.... have seventy-two weeks
With their own calendar.

On the fifth day, the needle pricks
To measure whether to cloister
Or venture out and roister
With the crowd
To hear the joyful noise –
Which now is loud.

On the fourth fifth,
The needle's prick portrays the marker
Of the trail being traveled
To delay or eradicate
The progression of the deadly cells.
Then tells it's time
To turn the page
To enter the next cycle-
 the next cage.

The poisonous trail begins again
With the slow flow of that
Which kills and saves
And staves off early demise.
Without a concise predict
Of damage done to what is left
Of health, but to go forward
With stealth to seek closure –
Week by week, day by day,
Without knowing the price to pay.

Seventeen months end,
The calendar continues its cost,
The current picture is colorful
Though much was lost.

2005 — 2013

It is not what is remembered
But what is chosen to forget.
To live with mortality
Is beset with trepidation,
While a better preparation
For life everlasting
Is to bet on normality
And remember to forget.

Compliment

You gave my spirits a lift,
Thanks for sending along the word.
I guess it disproves the adage
About being seen, not heard.

Is loveliness next to Godliness?
If so, I need more than just a share,
But perhaps I can be pretty, peppy
   and cute
When I get back my hair!

Unresolved Question for the Second Watch

Ishmael once again has taken his bite
Leaving me with questions – left and right.

The mane has gone
Down the drain
In huge pieces .and
I could resurrect
The cranial prosthesis
As the dome is still
Not cubic….
But what do I do
About the brows
…and the pubic?

Side Effects Amended

I have finished the fourth,
My CA125 registers eleven,
This makes me smile,
I've postponed heaven…
At least for a while.

I have now had the fifth.
My constitution feels like hell—
My legs ache, the nausea rolls,
The energy's gone, the ankles swell,
The digestion has slowed
To the pace of a snail.

I've taken Tylenol, Anzemet,
Phillips M of M
But the shark says
I can't stop him.

He said, "You were the wife of a lawyer,
And also the mother,
You had another for a brother.
You should have listened
To your kin and kith,
Bad things happen
From taking the fifth!"

Side Effects

My platelets have plunged
My energy lapsed
It would seem
I need a nap,
Perchance to dream....

What are these eerie figures
that through my eyes do peek?
A Manx, a fox, a carriion crow's beak.
They drift in my head
What shadows they cast
(Wouldn't they give friend Freud a blast?)

I have three more months
of this inanity,
Then with luck, I'll return
To a modicum of sanity.

Side Effect #2

My memory fades
(It may be age)
My mind wanders
Off the page.

I can no longer
Concentrate
Don't know the place
Don't know the date.

I have become
Quite inane.
The doctor says
It's chemo brain.

Alienation

I look in the mirror
and bewail my fate,
I have no brows, no lashes,
There's no hair on my pate.

I used to look in the mirror
and see my mother's face
Now another has taken her place
I look in the mirror and no
longer see me,
There's the grandmother
Of the alien E.T.!!

The Yew and Me

My ancestral blue blood
Is now mixed with platinum
And juice of the yew.
What that does to my nobility,
I haven't a clue.

I do know, though,
They played havoc
With my bones,
But if they are getting
Those low-life cancer cells,
I'd claim kin with
Pacman Jones!!

The Second Watch - Problem Solving

Dr. Jones' shark has taken its toll,
It's left me not joyous, but droll
Since once again all my hair it stole.

The mane has gone
Down the drain
In huge pieces...
I've resurrected the old
Cranial Prosthesis,
As the dome did not turn to cubic.

I've re-painted the eyebrows,
And found a fig leaf
For the pubic!!

Goody Two Shoes

Though the Big C's
  In remission
The trepidation
  doesn't stop,
I keep waiting…
….waiting…
For the other shoe
  to drop.

Chemogate

The chemo stole my hair, my legs,
 All of my fingers hurt,
I have a wig, a cane,
I can't button my shirt.

My blood count is low,
I have no immunity,
  But this I can say
   With some impunity:
      Though the toxin took its toll
       Of my time's raveled sleeve,
         With a vengeance I hold
           To my joie de vivre…

A Sonnet*

Life has dealt me a new little death –
  It's not my first walk in this place -
  I pause to catch a breath
And try to compose my face.
  I scavenge for a resurrection-

Grief is hard to abort-
  I must change direction,
Not waste time that's short.
  Looking at what's offered me:
  The wonders of the cosmic world,
  Family and friends - love that's free,
 The glory the seasons make,
  New knowledge kindling what I see,

Resurrection's there to take.

* Upon learning the cancer was back

Doggerel

Some Doctor Doggerel

There was a lady with guile
Who had a porcelain smile
It's utterly fantastic
Her hips are both plastic
Her hair is a nylon pile.

In her ear a battery does rest
Another keeps pace in her chest
I do not impugn
The angioplasty balloon
But protest the silicone breast.

Her eyes hold hydrophilic lens
And collagen lifts both chins,
I'm not supercilic,
Her knees are acrylic
Her shins are aluminum pins.

This guileful lady I do not reject,
For her surgeons I feel much respect,
But- while her parts are now tradeable
They are not biodegradable,
I expect she's not politically correct!!

A Gift

You say I make many mistakes,
I say, yes I do.
They are a present to enhance
The perfection of you.

Automation

When I take my car to a mechanic
--and this happens without fail -
He treats me like some dumb bimbo,
As if all automotive data is lodged
In the prized organ of the male.

Garrulous Guest

Loquacious is a lovely sounding word,
A dialogue however, is better.
A chance to agree or contradict,
Listening or speaking ,
A chance to choose and pick.

 But words stored in the cerebrum,
As if held back by a cable,
Break free – become a monologue-
Unabridgedly flooding the table.
Seeking all ears,
Ending all speaking.

Medic-Care

I have a band of Medics
Orchestrating my demise,
The conductor is my Internist
And although I think he's wise,
I find it very hard
To obey
The gynecologist
Pathologist
Oncologist
Dermatologist
Ophthalmologist
Cardiologist
And
Physiologist.
Sometimes I wish
They'd just leave it up to God.

My friends say to me
They'll never go that far,
It's not the Hippocratic oath
That's who they think they are....

They have handed me a new note—
I must free my days
Of stress and strife—
Now I need a psychologist to orchestrate
My life!

Tech's Lex

A blackberry was a fruit,
  used for jam and pie;
A byte was done with teeth,
  spelled with an 'i'.
But the 'i' has gone to phone,
  to pod, pad- to an Apple's core.
In age, I've grown quite contrary;
  I do abhor
The new vocabulary.

A ram will remain a sheep,
A tweet, a chirp from a chickadee;
If I use a kindle, it will be I need
To light the logs
That I may sit, and turn
 The pages of a book I yearn
    to read.
 And though my memory may be
    at its dregs
I recall a laptop is made
    of knees and legs!

Experiences

Writing

When I compose prose
It's building a house.
First, the blueprints – a plan –
A hope to land on solid ground-
Not a house built on sand.
I start construction
Laying line after line-
   Humor or facts.
When I finish,
It's my decision
To open the door,
Let you in
To my labor of precision.

When I write a poem
I hold a brush in hand -
The medium - my feelings -
Spontaneity – my plan.
Guided by intuition,
I pull the colors needed to start.
Whether the results are
Success or failure,
It's a labor of the heart.

Absurd Words

I do not writer with obscurity
To convince you I am profound,
Sometimes I write with absurdity
As I search for a relevant sound.

Now, I CAN write obscurely,
And surely there's some profundity
In the absurd seen in a lifetime.
But essential as air – somewhere -
There has to be a rhyme.

The Color of Tears

You are light
I am dark
But no matter,
Whether you are
Rich or poor
Young or old,
Regardless of gender,
When we claim
The red, white and blue
    draped 'cargo'–
their last surrender –
Our tears are the same.

**Upon learning four young men were killed in Afghanistan
    And seeing on TV the plane bringing them home , and the
    Reporter calling the bodies "cargo".*

Alienation

Some of my friends have grandeur
Some hold this image quite dear
Some wish I, too, were a grandee
But it is perfectly clear
I can never a silk purse be –
For even with decorative
   embellishment-
I remain simply me..

Hope

Hope is the start of a prayer
Nestled in the heart
Holding hands with faith
Warding off despair.

Choices

I have watched attorneys at work,
some a part of my day,
I see their tenacious tact -
Without an iota of rue -
Of bending our brain
To gain-say the fact
as we're led to their view.

I have known artists
Of the brush and the pen -
Also a part of my day -
They lend us a sight
Of the dark and light
 open our mind and eye
That we then may decide
Whether to laugh, cry,
      Accept or deny.

Blind — Sighted

I'm driven by unanswered questions,
Ignorance drives my mind
The more I know,
The more I know I don't know.
Leaving solutions I must find.

While the sphere widens
My brain keeps going around,
As I continue learning –
My ignorance becomes profound.

Legacy

I have been chosen again
to stay.

I watch you unpack
for your journey
and fill your file folders
with folderol.
My spirit unravels like
a ball of yarn, frayed with rage.

My only gift for your journey
is an infinite faith,
which sometimes burns dimly
like a green limb on the hearth's fire,
That was stoked by you.

I wonder as I watch
if these fingers will thaw,
these palms warm,
To once more rewind the yarn.

Rebirth

As I settle within myself -
A movement that makes me whole.
Reclaiming my self-respect,
I reflect about this goal.

Achieving a valuable victory,
   - Winning over the pain.
Letting go the sin of pride
   And rejection's knife,
Not expecting a reward
   Of happiness,
But rewinding the thread of life.

Syntax

We sit at the kitchen counter
We speak of many things –
From Genesis to Darwin,
Hitchens and Bishop Spong,
Wendell Berry and Ginsberg
Right and wrong, war and peace -
Even Jason and his quest
   for the Golden Fleece.

Flavored with our unremitting
    maternal cords
We search to resolve the tensions
Between the heart and mind,
Feeling more joy in the interchange
Than the answers we fail to find.

Reconciliation at Hilton Head

They spent the week-end
  - perhaps their last -
Without reasoning,
Only exhaustive obsessions
With the past.

The sun beat hot
At the water's edge
To dredge reflections
Of what was, for them
What would ever be.

They waded toward the current,
Aware of what was meant;
Made a seawall of the stones -
Stones to toss into the waves
    As the tide went out.

The Gift of This Day

I raised my arms
Then lifted my face
To feel the warmth
Of summer's embrace.

I stopped to contemplate
The multi-colored transformate
Of autumn's oaks dropping their leaves
As if it were I they wished to please.

I held tight my coat
Against the rain and snowy days
That chilled my hands, my throat,
Aware of winter's wily ways.

The dogwood's crosses are white
The spirea bows to spring,
I feast both eyes and ears
As the wren begins to sing.

With eighty-plus years of wonder
Each new season's gives a lift,
I'm still amazed at their glory,
Thankful for each day's gift.

Quatrains of Questions

The Greatest of These is Faith?

For some faith comes easy
For others, it's quite hard;
If you search for a beginning,
Ultimately you find God.

The Greatest of These is Hope?

You may see your brother's hunger,
See his need for love and praise,
But without the possibility of promise
Indifference becomes malaise.

The Greatest of these is Charity?

"Now abideth faith, hope, charity,
　these three;
But the greatest of these is charity"
Yet compassion becomes as nothing
Without a community of solidarity.

And then there was Love —

Love outlasts death
Love survives the dust,
Love fills your pockets,
You love because you must.

Misson

Some say...
I'm a piece of a star
From a cosmic force
On an orderly course.

Others -
I'm made from dust
Or from a rib, as some say -
On the sixth day.

But whether I twinkle
As part of a plan,
Or in His image
 rule over the land
 I am a prolific sensation
Fulfilling a responsibility
  Of continuing creation.

Love Song

You throw open your throat,
Puff out your chest,
There comes a note
Lovely as Puccini.
You await an answer -
A song from on high -
Then without taking a bow,
……Away you fly…. ..

Family and Friends

My Mother

My mother never
Sang all the songs that were in her
Never danced the tunes that tapped her toes

Born of an era
Where home was a woman's palace
Her portals were from the back porch
To the parlor
To the pillars facing the lawn.

With a fiefdom of five
To feed and clothe
Her day began at dawn
   To tend the children,
        the chickens
         the peonies
        the peaches
         the cherries
        my father had grown..

My mother never
Patronized the "colored"
Who helped tend
      the children,
       the chickens,
        and the cherries

They became friends – her shed
From loneliness.

But still the music played on –
In her head.

Sometimes she would sit and sigh –
the laughter that filled our lives would quiet-
Stoop to pick a little one to her lap
To teach a rhyme,
        to read,
         to write,
        to subtract and add,
Stretching the time
For the song to die

Sometimes she picked up her guitar
And "Red River Valley" would flow,
Sometimes the piano was where
We heard the songs
Of places she dreamed to go.

My mother never
Sang for my father

When he arrived with small black bag,
His coat flung over his arm,
Eager to get to his orchard
To oversee the farm,
She hurriedly pushed in a stray hair pin,
Told us to behave,
Her face began to glow—
Now, her day would begin.

My mother never
Believed he loved her
As she loved him.

I thought so.

Encounter at the Post Office

Her hair was brown and long,
   Hung down her back,
Her cheeks uncrossed by wires.
She hummed a song and
   Engaged in banter
With the man behind the counter,
Unaware that I was there.

We had come to post the mail –
I, white hair bristling like
The spores of a dandelion,
A quilted face, moving with
   The pace of a snail—
Watched, stung by memory
I knew her, she didn't know me.

I once touched lives, hand by hand,
And then change came.
I say to her, "Sing and shine,
Claim the name of youth,
Be minimally indiscreet,
For change will come
And you will tread my street."

Mary Margaret's Hands

Small chubby hands beating a tune
On the high chair's tray
Using a spoon, then
Imperiously throwing it away..

Little hands pouring lemonade tea
In my demitasse cup
Chatting, gossiping, two busy bodies
With peanut butter and jelly
To fill them up.

Fingers coloring with purple, green
Intent on yellow and blue.
As if they knew then
What they were destined to do.

Across the polished table
Long fingers tipped in red
With bracelets to merrily swing,
Waiting to cheer with friends
Waiting for the phone to ring..

Hands at my table disappear
To seek a knowledge
Not found here.
Then back, slim and smooth
To leave once more
To use their talents on a distant shore.

I long to reach across the table
And restrain the hands that hold
Some small part of me
And all the years now spent
But this can never be.

Knowing these hands are hers alone,
I fold mine in my lap
Exalting in what they will discover
Knowing they will grasp life's truths
And should they falter,
They will recover..

For Katherine on Oct. First

We are the old ones, Katherine
With spacey heads and posture bent;
We have lent the best of us
   To those who come.
We manage their ludicrous attitudes
  And callous platitudes
    From the shelf,
Continuing to look for happiness
 In the face of age, illness
    and death itself.

May 31, ?

My mother called me "Sparkle Plenty,"
My sister thought I was a curse
Some friends think I'm smart
Some say smart-aleck or worse.

Now, I'm not bi-polar
Not schizophrenic say I,
It's just that my Zodiac sign,
Is the two-faced Gemini!

Cathedra

My father said to me,
"My orchard is my temple;
the fruit it will bear
is proof enough
That Someone is living there."

Why should he go
To bricks and mortar
To seek a knowing seer
When the One known best
To him, lived very near?

Pat's Poetry

Her magic is almost surreal
She catches a moment in ink.
The challenge of a few short lines,
Makes you think, no-o-o, feel.

I'm caught in her silk twine,
I struggle to pull out the heart
—let the words wash over me –
Suddenly, the moment is mine.

Life Everlasting — for Marilyn

One who is blessed
With a zest for living
Finds joy in others,
Generous and giving,
Thinks first of helping
  others to thrive
Owns immortality
While still alive.

Parental Control

Nourished by nerves and adrenalin,
Dressed in the Thrift Shop's old,
I came to roast Bill
   With fun stories to be told
To a stalwart three hundred
    Of his friends.

But where was she?
She promised she would come
She said she would…..
Then I caught a glimpse
Of a slim black dress
Pearls at the neck and ear
Smooth hair and face
Eyes scanning the room—
Oblivious to my latent fear—
To place herself to see and hear.

Trepidation fled with her arrival,
I approached the podium with ease
   for Bill, for her, and to please
   the crowd whose money went to St. Luke's
To serve "the least of these".

As I thanked each guest
She quietly approached,
Gave me this gift….
"Mom, you were the best"..
I felt my spirits shift.

Two Faces
for Pat

I, too, have known ecstasy,
I have also known despair,
If I had a voice
My choice would be
The joy that's heaven sent.

But grief seeps in –
Unwelcome, unasked -
And I retreat, masked,
That I not greet you
With winter's discontent.

Yes, I have been without hope,
And I have known much bliss –
Neither of which
Do I easily dismiss.

Salute to My Daughter

She speaks in hyperbole
A shower is "pouring down rain"
A passing car was" going a hundred"
A bruised finger is "killing me"…

On the other hand,
She is multi-talented
Full of the joy of living –
Gracious and forgiving,
She hurts when others hurt,
Her heart is warm and huge.

So no matter if
She does exaggeratedly speak –
 a drizzle or deluge –
It's her company we enjoy,
Her voice we seek

Victor Judge

I wanted
To be judged rather than judged not
To have my subjective, self-revealing ramblings
Looked at with a critical eye,
Correcting the errors, the spelling, the syntax
Even though I may bristle and sigh.

I received
An astonishment at what he can retain,
An abounding memory, an incomparable insight,
An ear attuned to the pitch of language,
A kindness never to disdain.
A knowledge of both poetry and prose,
Encouragement to keep us working,
To write of nothing or more profoundly,
Expressing whatever each knows.

And he
Accepted my endeavor to write
Even if I fell short
Of the high standards
Of Strunk and White.

The Family Tree

When the season's chartreuse changes to white
The Dogwood chases the Cherry and the Pear
And the breeze vacuums the carpet
  Of Spring Beauties under the trees,
Then grief swarms over me like angry bees.

But not that time – not that day.
We had gathered for a family portrait
Under a canopy of blossoms on my daughter's lawn
Dressed in their Sunday best
They all came at my request.

I sat in the midst of thirteen
Like a pistil in the petals of a bloom.
The patriarch, untimely stroked by fate,,
Beginning his fall from the tree,
Took his place by me.

The other men stood by him,
All dressed in Brooks Brothers dark,
With bright ties and black knee socks,
  In sartorial splendor – their usual style,
And for the picture, each practiced his smile.

The young boys in navy blue blazers,
The girls, preening in their pastels,
The women dressed with their usual panache,
The youngest on his father's arm
In smocked jumper, exuded a two-year's charm

All awaited the cue to say 'cheese' –
Only the teen-age boy with a frown –
Laughed, teased and joked for the celluloid
No one, that day, aware of the fact,
It would be the last with the family intact.

Nowadays, when I pause at my desk
  And touch each face,
I feel the stinger in my breast
But remember the love that was,
Filled with pride in what is, and will be,
And turn my gaze to the blossoms of the tree.

CPSIA information can be obtained at www.ICGtesting.com
Printed in the USA
LVOW06*1741071013

355823LV00003B/24/P